5/07

Living in
Australia

Written and photographed by
David Hampton

SEA-TO-SEA

Mankato Collingwood London

Bogota Public Library
375 Larch Avenue
Bogota, NJ 07603

This edition first published in 2007 by
Sea-to-Sea Publications
1980 Lookout Drive
North Mankato
Minnesota 56003

Copyright © Sea-to-Sea Publications 2007

Printed in China

All rights reserved

Library of Congress Cataloging-in-Publication Data

Hampton, David.
    Australia / by David Hampton.
        p. cm.-- (Living in--)
    Includes index.
    ISBN-13: 978-1-59771-041-1
    1. Australia--Juvenile literature. 2. Australia--Social life and customs--Juvenile
    literature. I. Title. II. Series.

DU96.H36 2006
994--dc22

                                                                    2005057547

9 8 7 6 5 4 3 2

Published by arrangement with the Watts Publishing Group Ltd, London

Series editor: Ruth Thomson
Series designer: Edward Kinsey
Additional photograph: Bridget Sherlock 8(c)

Contents

4   This is Australia

6   Canberra—the capital

8   Famous sights

10 Living in cities

12 Living in the outback

14 Working in the outback

16 A sports nation

18 Shopping

20 On the move

22 Family life

24 Time to eat

26 School time

28 Having fun

30 Going further

31 Glossary

32 Index

This is Australia

Australia is the only country in the world that is also a continent. It is a huge island surrounded by sea. Tasmania, a small island off the south coast, is also part of Australia.

The country is divided into eight regions—six states and two territories. Tasmania is one of the states.

△**Rain forest**
Rain forest covers vast areas of northern Queensland. Some is being cut down to make way for farming and mining.

△**Desert**
Much of the west and center of Australia is desert or semidesert, with vast salt pans. Less than 20 inches (500 mm) of rain falls there per year.

▷**Cities**
Seven of the biggest cities are on the coast. These are the capitals of the seven states.

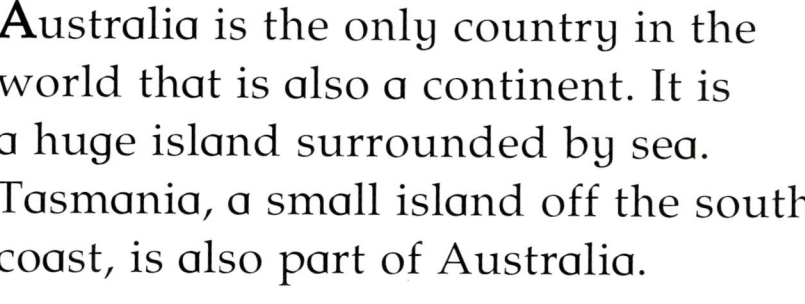

Fact Box

Capital: Canberra
Population: 18.5 million
Official language: English
Main religion: Christianity
Highest mountain: Mount Kosciusko (7,310 ft/2,228 m)
Longest river: Darling (1,702 miles/2,739 km))
State capitals: Sydney, Perth, Melbourne, Brisbane, Adelaide, Hobart
Territory capitals: Canberra, Darwin
Currency: Australian dollar

This is Australia

△People
The Aborigines are the first known inhabitants of Australia. Since the first Europeans arrived in 1788, people from more than 200 countries have made Australia their home.

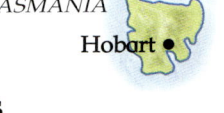

◁Coral reefs
There are coral reefs off the western and eastern coastlines. The largest is the Great Barrier Reef.

◁Mountains
The Blue Mountains, west of Sydney, are often covered with cloud. The water vapor in the air makes them appear blue.

5

Canberra–the capital

Canberra is the capital of Australia. This small city was built from scratch in the early 1900s as the new place of government. Before this, Melbourne had been the capital. Canberra was designed by an American architect, who won a competition to create this new city.

△**The Australian crest**
A kangaroo and an emu, the national animal and bird, are part of the crest of Australia.

▷**Parliament House**
The government meets in Parliament House, which was built in 1988. The old Parliament building is now the National Portrait Gallery.

△**Aboriginal embassy**
This building, near the old Parliament, is a reminder that the Aborigines are unhappy about the way they are treated by the mainly white government.

Canberra—the capital

▷**Lake Burley Griffin**
This manmade lake is named after the architect who planned the city. It was created by damming a nearby river.

▽**War memorial**
This building is a tribute to the 102,600 people who have died in wars while serving their country.

▷**A view of the city**
The view of the capital from Mount Ainslie is popular with the thousands of tourists who visit Canberra every year.

Famous sights

Australia is famous for its unique wildlife, especially marsupials, such as the kangaroo, wallaby, and koala.

The country is also well known for its fantastic beaches, unusual landscape, and friendly people, as well as for important Aboriginal landmarks.

△**Aboriginal art**
There are Aboriginal cave paintings in the Kakadu National Park in the Northern Territory. Some are thought to be more than 20,000 years old.

△**Koala**
The koala is a nocturnal mammal that lives in forests. It eats only the leaves of one species of eucalyptus tree.

Baby kangaroo (joey)

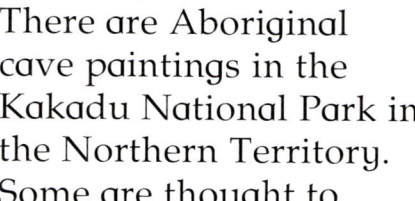

◁**Uluru**
Uluru (Ayers Rock) rises from the flat desert about 155 miles (250 km) from Alice Springs. It is a sacred site for Aborigines. It appears to change color throughout the day.

Famous sights

△**Bondi beach**
Bondi is Sydney's most famous beach. People come here from all over the world to surf on the waves that roll in from the Tasman Sea.

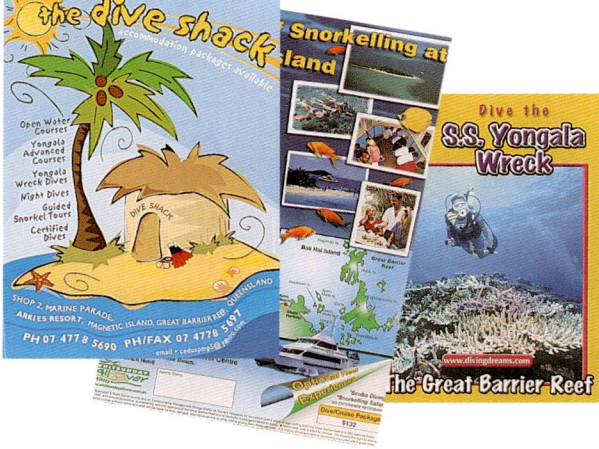

◁**The Great Barrier Reef**
The Great Barrier Reef is a huge tourist attraction. People dive and snorkel around the reef, watching the schools of tropical fish.

△**Sydney Opera House**
The Sydney Opera House is a series of concert halls and theaters. It stands overlooking Sydney Harbor. Its shape was inspired by seashells.

9

Living in cities

Almost nine out of ten Australians live in towns or cities, and within 50 miles (80 km) of the sea. Most families own houses in the suburbs. The houses are usually detached, built of brick, and have large yards. In recent years, high-rise apartments have been built near city centers for people who want to live close to where they work.

△**The police**
Each state has its own police force. This policeman patrols the park in a vehicle that has a sunshade.

△**Suburbs**
Most cities are very spread out. Yards have tall trees to provide shade for homes.

◁**Town houses**
New homes often have huge balconies or verandahs where people can sit out. To save space, houses may have a garage with space for two cars underneath.

Living in cities

△**Cell phones**
Business people use cell phones to keep in touch with their office wherever they are.

△**City centers**
Banks, offices, restaurants, department stores, and other outlets are concentrated in city centers. The streets are crowded at lunchtimes and at rush hours.

Brochures for city sights

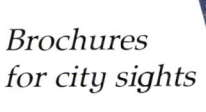

11

Living in the outback

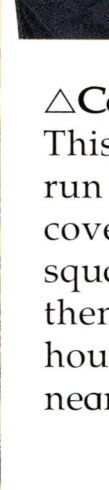

Australians call the countryside the *bush* or the *outback*. Very few people live here. In hot, dry places, few crops can grow and fresh water is scarce.

Properties and towns may be hundreds of miles apart.

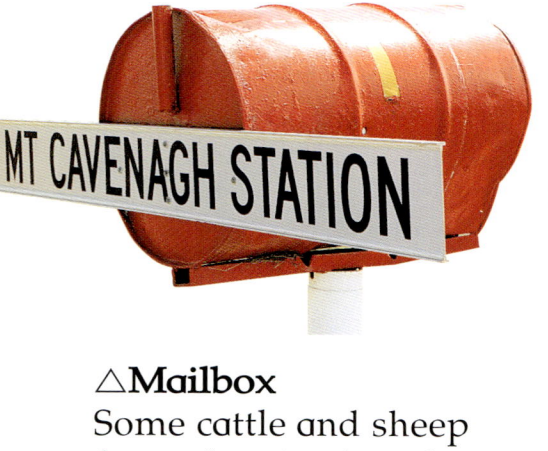

△Mailbox
Some cattle and sheep farms (*stations*) in the remotest parts of the outback have mailboxes as far as 95 miles away from the house.

▷Homesteads
Most farmhouses (*homesteads*) are built of timber with corrugated iron roofs. Outbuildings house workers who come to help farmers at busy times of year, such as sheep shearing.

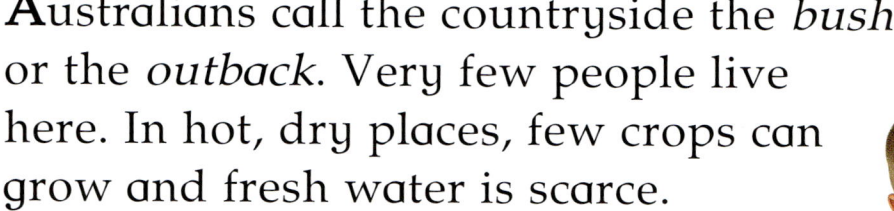

△Cattle ranching
This man and his family run a cattle station that covers thousands of square miles. It takes them more than six hours to drive to the nearest town.

Living in the outback

◁**Collecting water**
This woman from the far north has to collect water from a spring a long walk from her home.

▽**Artesian water**
Outback homes mainly rely on water pumped up from underground by windmills. The water is warm and salty. It must be filtered before it can be drunk.

△**An outback town**
Many people visit town only a few times a year. They stock up with packaged foods. Most of them travel in an all-terrain vehicle, called a utility (*ute*).

▽**Flying Doctor Service**
Distances between places in the outback are so great that planes are used to take people to the hospital in an emergency.

13

Working in the outback

Most people in the outback work in either farming or mining.

Farmers mainly keep sheep or cattle. Cereal crops, especially wheat, and fruit, such as apples and oranges, are grown for export.

Sheepskin boot

Sugar refinery

△Sheep
Australia is home to about 150 million sheep. It is the world's biggest exporter of wool and meat.

▷Cattle
These cattle in the Northern Territory are being taken to market. This is a long, hard, hot, and dusty job for the horseback riders.

△Sugar
Sugarcane, grown in Queensland, is one of Australia's most important crops. Many towns have a refinery where the cane is processed into sugar.

Working in the outback

▽▷Grapes

Grapes, grown in the south and east, are mostly used for wine. These grapes are being dried in the sun and will be packaged as raisins.

△Loading up

This huge truck is being loaded with bauxite. This will be smelted and used to make aluminum.

Iron ore

Bauxite

Lead ore

Mining

Iron and lead ore, bauxite, silver, gold, and coal are dug from Australia's many mines, along with precious diamonds and opals. These are exported all over the world.

A sports nation

Because the weather is usually warm, Australians take part in all sorts of outdoor sports. They are particularly good at water sports, like swimming, sailing, and windsurfing. In 2000, Sydney hosted the Olympic Games.

△*Aussie Rules*
This popular game combines the rules of soccer and rugby. There are 18 players on each side.

▷Tennis
Children take tennis lessons from a young age. These boys are coached three nights a week and play matches on weekends.

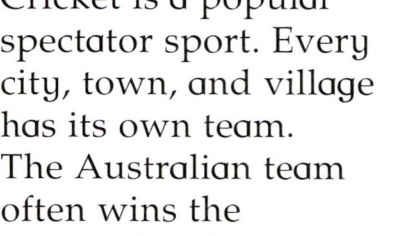

△Cricket
Cricket is a popular spectator sport. Every city, town, and village has its own team. The Australian team often wins the International Test Match series.

16

A sports nation

▷Surf lifesaving
Most beaches have a lifesaving club. Members take turns watching for people in trouble. The clubs hold races in the surf kayaks used for rescue.

▽Beach flags
Brightly colored flags indicate where it is safest to swim or surf.

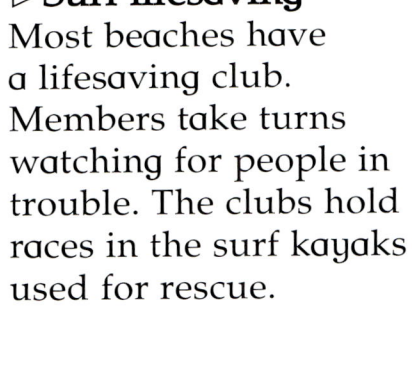

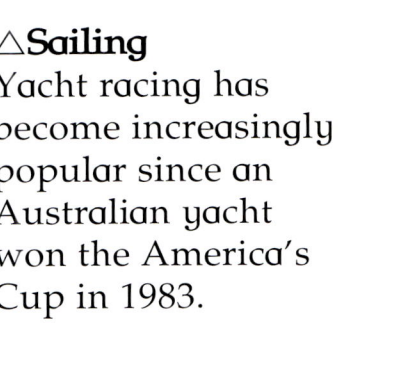

△Sailing
Yacht racing has become increasingly popular since an Australian yacht won the America's Cup in 1983.

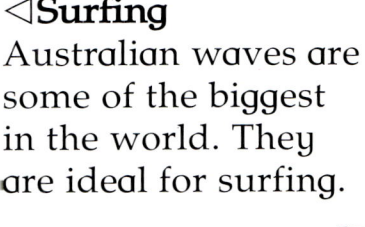

◁Surfing
Australian waves are some of the biggest in the world. They are ideal for surfing.

Shopping

Towns still have many stores on the main streets. In cities, these are being replaced by out-of-town shopping centers or shopping malls. The wide range of stores and products reflects the differing tastes and lifestyles of the multicultural population.

△**Shopping streets**
Stores often have flat roofs that extend over the sidewalk. These protect shoppers from both sun and rain.

△**Markets**
On weekends, street markets are a feature of many towns and cities. Hot food and snacks are often available there, too.

▷**Fruit stores**
Fruit is almost entirely homegrown. Tropical fruits, such as bananas, pineapples, and mangoes, grow in the north and east.

Pineapple

Shopping

▽Homegrown food
All these products come from crops grown on the rich farmlands of the east coast.

Tomato sauce

Canned fruit

Orange juice

Yeast extract

△Grocery stores
In cities, it is quite common to see Chinese, Greek, Indian, and Jewish grocery stores side by side in the same street.

Dollars

Cents

△Australian currency
Australians use dollars and cents.

△▷Convenience stores
Convenience stores sell candies, lottery tickets, phone cards, and newspapers, as well as food. Foreign language newspapers are sold in all big cities.

Phone card

Lottery tickets

Candies

On the move

Transportation systems are very modern and well organized. Major roads link the major cities of every state. Most families own two cars.

Melbourne, Adelaide, and Brisbane have trams. Sydney has a monorail.

△**Trains**
Trains are still used to carry freight, but, because of the huge distances, most people fly from city to city.

△**City roads**
New highways link the suburbs to city centers. These help the flow of traffic in and out of the cities.

◁**Monorail**
The monorail in the center of Sydney links the shopping and business districts.

On the move

Kulgera	18
Erldunda	94
Alice Springs	293
Darwin	1780

Distance sign

◁Road or runway?
In times of emergency, some roads in the outback double as runways for the Royal Flying Doctor Service.

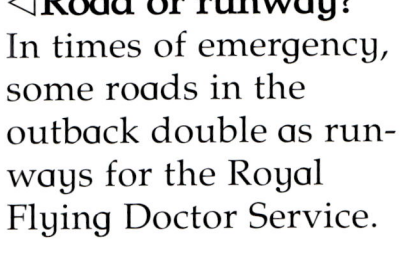

The National Highway
The Federal Government ...Funcing Better Roads

CAUTION
ROAD TRAINS
50 METRES LONG

▽A road train
Huge trucks with three linked trailers move goods across the country. A road train can transport hundreds of sheep or cattle at a time.

Roads in the outback
The distances between places in the outback can be enormous. There is very little traffic on the roads, so most roads only have a single lane.

Family life

Most families enjoy a comfortable way of life. Their homes are spacious and well equipped with fridges, freezers, and other modern appliances.

People work hard in the week, but rarely on weekends. Families enjoy spending their time off together.

▽**Watching television**
Almost every family has a television and watching sport is very popular. The Australian soaps, *Home and Away* and *Neighbors,* are watched worldwide.

Weekly TV magazine

△**Swimming pools**
Many homes have enough space in the backyard for a large swimming pool.

Family life

▷**Bedrooms**
Modern homes have at least four bedrooms and two bathrooms. Children usually have their own room.

◁**Drying clothes**
Washing never takes long to dry in the warm climate, especially in the north and west, where temperatures can reach 104° F.

△**Computers**
Children often do their homework on a computer. They use e-mail to correspond with friends and relations abroad.

▷**Texting**
People text their friends on their cell phones. Phone charges are very low compared with those in most other developed countries.

23

Time to eat

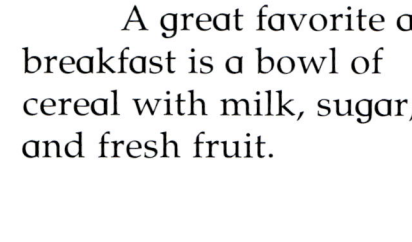

A traditional Australian meal includes meat, vegetables, and a dessert. People now eat dishes from all over the world, however, especially those from different parts of Asia. The city of Sydney claims that visitors could eat in a different ethnic restaurant every day of the year, without ever eating food from the same place twice!

△ **Breakfast**
A great favorite at breakfast is a bowl of cereal with milk, sugar, and fresh fruit.

▷ **Barbecues**
People take advantage of the warm climate and eat outside as often as possible. They cook steak, lamb, or fish over hot charcoal on a barbecue (*barbie*).

△ **Barbecue food**
Barbecues aren't complete without a selection of fresh salads, chips, and a plate of chocolate brownies.

24

Time to eat

Meat pie

△ Take-out food
Meat pies are the traditional snack. These are being replaced by foods from around the world. (Roast *chooks* are roast chicken.)

▽ Restaurants
Eating out is very informal. Cafés and restaurants often have outside seating. In big cities, there are ethnic restaurants of all kinds.

△ Snack bars
City commuters often start their day with coffee and cakes at a snack bar.

▷ Fish
There is a plentiful supply of fresh fish, such as tuna and mullet. Shellfish are farmed off the coast. Tiger shrimp are a favorite—they only turn pink when they are cooked.

Cooked tiger shrimp

Raw tiger shrimp

Bogota Public Library
375 Larch Avenue
Bogota, NJ 07603

25

School time

Education in Australia is free. It is compulsory for most children between the ages of 5 and 15. However, some Aboriginal parents choose not to send their children to state schools. Instead, they educate them in the traditions of their own culture at home.

▽In class

Lessons begin at 8.30 or 9 a.m. and continue until 3 or 3.30 p.m. There are always activities and sports after school.

△Going to school

Children who live near school may walk or cycle there. Many schools provide locked, covered bike racks for cyclists.

◁School buses

Children who live a long way from school may have to get up early to catch a school bus. The ride may take up to an hour.

School time

◁ Learning outside

When they have lessons outside, children have to wear hats to protect them from the hot sun.

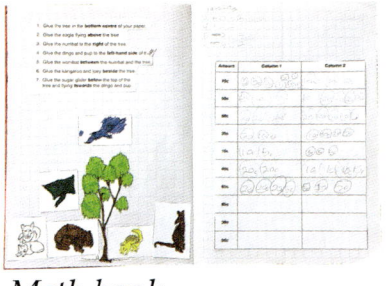

Math book

Learning at a distance

In the remote outback, some children are taught over the radio by the School of the Air. Each pupil has a radio set at home and talks for up to five hours a day to the teacher and other pupils. Children, parents, and teachers meet several times a year to discuss the pupils' progress.

◁△ The School of the Air

In 2001, the School of the Air celebrated its 50th anniversary.

27

Having fun

Australians are a particularly fun-loving nation. They enjoy the outdoor life and almost everything they do in their spare time reflects this. There are national parks in every state. These are a popular place to spend time hiking or exploring during the long school vacations in the summer (around Christmastime).

△**Camping**
There are camping and caravan sites all over Australia. These are well used, especially on the weekends.

△**Beach volleyball**
Teams, especially life-saving teams, play volleyball on the beach. Running in soft sand helps them stay in shape.

▷**Fishing**
Fishing for sport is popular both in the sea and on rivers. The freshly caught fish are cooked on barbecues.

Sun lotion

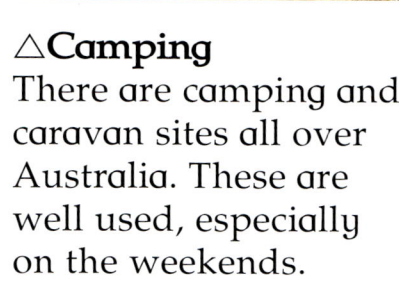

Sunglasses

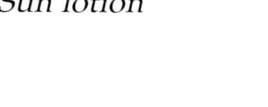

△**Sun protection**
The sun can be very hot, so people are careful to put on sun lotion and wear sunglasses.

28

Having fun

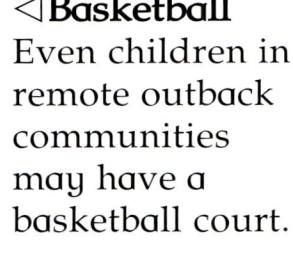

△**Cycling**
Families use mountain bikes to explore the rugged landscape.

◁**Basketball**
Even children in remote outback communities may have a basketball court.

△**Amusement parks**
People enjoy daredevil rides in city amusement parks.

Going further

Aboriginal painting

Lots of Aboriginal paintings are made by using the end of a stick instead of a brush.

Look closely at the boomerang and use the same painting technique to make your own pictures and designs.

Candy wrappers

The Australian candy bars below each feature a different Australian animal.

Design some candy wrappers, using a different Australian theme, for example, sports or famous sights.

A fire poster

Fire is one of the greatest dangers to life and property in Australia.

Design a poster to encourage people not to light fires when the weather is very hot and dry.

Websites

www.about-australia.com
www.frogandtoad.com.au
www.auslig.gov.au

Glossary

Artesian water Water that has been taken from underground.

Commuter Someone who travels some distance from home to work each day.

Continent One of the large landmasses of the world.

Coral reef A bank of coral just below sea level.

Crest An official badge.

Currency The money used in a country.

Exporter Someone who sells a product from one country to another.

Marsupial A mammal that carries its young in a pouch.

Monorail A railroad with only one rail.

Nocturnal Active at night.

Ore A solid, rocklike material that contains a valuable metal.

Population The number of people who live in one place.

Rain forest A lush, dense forest found in hot regions with high rainfall.

Refinery A place where raw materials are turned into a product.

Smelt To melt ore to extract metal from it.

State A region of a country that has its own government for local affairs.

Suburbs Housing on the outer areas of a city.

Territory A region of a country that has its own government for local affairs, like a state.

Verandah A covered space along the side of a building.

Index

Page numbers in *italics* refer to entries in the fact box, on the map, or in the glossary.

Aborigines 5, 6, 8, 26, 30
Adelaide *4, 5,* 20
Alice Springs *5,* 8
amusement parks 29
animals 6, 8, 30
Aussie Rules 16
Ayers Rock *See* Uluru

barbecues 24, 28
bauxite 15
beaches 8, 9, 17, 28
bicycles 26, 29
Brisbane *4, 5,* 20
buses 26

camping 28
Canberra *4, 5,* 6, 7
cars 20
cattle 14, 21
cattle stations 12
cave paintings 8
cell phones 11, 23
children 23, 26, 27
Christianity *4*
cities 4, 6, 7, 10, 11, 20, 29
coal 15
computers 23
continent 4, *31*
coral reefs 5, *31*

crest 6, *31*
crops 14, 19
currency *4,* 19, *31*

Darwin *4, 5*
desert *4,* 8
diamonds 15

families 20, 22, 23, 29
farmers 12, 14
fire 30
fish 9, 24, 25
Flying Doctor Service 13, 21
food 13, 18, 19, 24, 25
fruit 14, 18

gold 15
government 6
grapes 15
Great Barrier Reef *5,* 9

Hobart *4, 5*
homesteads 12
homes 10, 12, 22, 23

lakes 7
life-saving clubs 17, 28

markets 14, 18
marsupial 8, *31*
meat 14, 24, 25
Melbourne *4, 5,* 6, 20
mining 14, 15

monorail 20, *31*
mountains *4,* 5

national parks 8, 28
New South Wales *5*
Northern Territory *5,* 8, 14

Olympic Games 16
opals 15
outback 12, 13, 14, 15, 21, 27

Parliament buildings 6
Perth *4, 5*
police 10

Queensland *4, 5,* 14

rain forest 4, *31*
refinery 14, *31*
restaurants 11, 24, 25
rivers *4, 5,* 7
road trains 21
roads 20, 21
runways 21

School of the Air 27
schools 26, 27
sheep 14, 21
sheep shearing 12
shops 11, 18, 19
silver 15
South Australia *5*
sports 9, 16, 17, 22, 26, 28, 29

state 4, *31*
suburbs 10, 20, *31*
surfing 9, 17
Sydney *4, 5,* 16, 20, 24
Sydney Harbor 9
Sydney Opera House 9

Tasmania *4, 5*
television 22
territory 4, *31*
tourists 7, 9
towns 10, 12, 13, 14, 18
traffic 20, 21
trains 20

Uluru *5,* 8
ute 13

Victoria *5*

water 13
Western Australia *5*
wine 15
wool 14